wildflowers in bloom

L U N A I R I S

author of
Dreaming in Purple

Disclaimer:

The writing contained in this book is an exaggeration of reality inspired by the author's own emotions, memories, dreams, and life experiences. Any relatable emotions brought forth by the reader are purely coincidence and are not the responsibility of the author.

! Trigger warning: content follows sensitive events regarding mental health, abuse (emotional, sexual) and vivid descriptions. May trigger relatable emotions. Please practice healthy self-care before, during, and after reading.
18+ Mature content warning: some of the content in this book may not be appropriate for young readers. Discretion is advised.

For more writing by LUNAIRIS
follow @lunairispoetry on Instagram.

ISBN: 978-1-9994921-2-0

wildflowers in bloom

the ascent into rebirth
is akin to falling
in love
beautiful
tragic
and blooming
with magic

CONTENTS

my memories lie pressed
between these pages
dried flowers once wild
now infinite, ageless
delicately preserved
beauty of the earth
I hope my colors
do not fade
first

wildflowers in bloom

a wildflower
is a woman
a free spirit who refuses
to be watered
to be planted
by none other than herself
she relies on
no man-made force
only nature's course
she grows
she lives
in the wild
with the wild
she blooms
by her own will
to survive

WILD FLOWER

you love the idea of a wild woman
but can you dance to her rhythmic silence
under a full moon
observe her as she releases
the cage around your heart
unexpected, suddenly soon

can you grasp her hand and follow
diving into an open field
of flowers and thorns
can you tangle yourself in her ivy
reach freedom together
without rendering her torn

would you clear the dirt
gently from her eyes
while cold hands
grasp the stems from the earth
can you kiss her passionately
with the sweet softness
of her petal's own rebirth

yes, you are bound to be marked
she is a nightshade in the dark
but us wildflower women
we blossom and bloom
from our wounds
by magic
of art

MOONFLOWERS

if wildflowers
were pressed into honey
sweet alchemy
would take place on my lips
my arms would embrace you
in a field of flowers
petals blooming
in light of a kiss
morning dew drops will glow
on our sunflower skin
as sol gives early rise
moonlight dancing on shadows
our bodies
planted in earth
in the night
moonflowers
revive

DISASTROUS

I am a reckless lover
with a lust for all things
beautiful and fragile
and I will love you
like a storm does
because
my heart
many times
has become one

I am also the lover
in the calm
that follows after
and I know
great monuments
are built
by the quake
of delightful
reckless
disaster

SCULPTED

do not let yourself
become too soft
so that others
become comfortable
trying to mold you
into something
you are not

you are not made of clay

You are the hardened heart of a masterpiece. It's taken years of your life being chipped away, eroded, rebuilt, and polished to turn yourself into a magnificent sculpture – a monumental survivor. Do not let yourself become too soft, so that others become comfortable with trying to mold you into something you are not. They hate who they are and cannot change themselves. You are not made of clay. You are the entire beauty and wonder of the earth.

4

Adrenaline

what if I told you
I quite enjoy
the wicked madness
you employ
would you drown me a little deeper
grasp my throat a little longer
burn your fires a little hotter
because I quite enjoy
the way it tickles under my feet
diving foolishly into your waters
pretending to drown into the deep
gives a thrill to us both
sadistic smiles
between the sheets
oh, I quite enjoy
dancing slowly to dry myself off
by the heat of your flames
I do not even mind the blood
boiling in my veins
or a match made even
wrestling you in chains
because I quite enjoy
your adrenaline
in the form
of a pleasurable pain
my darling
I quite enjoy
writhing on the floor
begging you
for more

DREADFUL

I once loved a man
who lived in darkness so much
it became him too

everyone he kissed
was given a taste of hell
behind an evil smile

the lucky ones, though
managed to escape alive
I am still burning

he keeps me trapped here
dragging me back when I run
I beg, let me go

UNBREAKABLE

I wore my power
like the armour
beneath my skin
the one thing
they could never
strip me of
or win

WITH THE RAVENS

let me fly with the ravens
blackened wings carry daggers
I am wild among them

circle prey with the ravens
we will soar – dive in for a thrill
I am free among them

shriek into night with the ravens
darkened mystery in our calling
I am safe among them

arise deathly omens with the ravens
vengeful visitors to traitors of truth
I am wise among them

let me fly with the ravens
caged midnight feathers no more
I am one among them

HOTWIRE

if ever you find yourself under fire
by someone foolishly playing
with live hot wires
do them a favor
fuse those two together
electrocuting them
as you rise higher

sparks will fly
what a show

SAVED

you were a man lost
until I found you in the dark
speaking nonsense to yourself, foolish
I took you by the hand
to calm your chaos, understand
darling
it made perfect sense
to me

I hear you

STONED TO DEATH

cast the first stone, sinner of more
who rules over salacious hell
your deeds will be punished
forevermore
frozen eternity you will dwell

stone me to death with your bloody hands
you are not so innocent yourself
as if every stone pelting my flesh
tore up your hate and projected it from hell

raise up another and aim straight for my heart
batter it and instead, tear yours apart
you are bruising darker than you know

stone me to death
I will raise them all up
fear in your eyes
as I have the last throw

my turn

PEACH FUZZ

I have had an aversion to my own body hair
since I could speak the words, "peach fuzz"
obsessively removing any speck of stubble
every single day from toe-tips to fingertips
and everywhere in between
long before I ever imagined
to groom myself for a man

what repulses me even more
is that some men think that we do this for them
as if they are entitled to our bodies
as if our bodily choices required their approval
as if we deserved to be accused of promiscuity
because of their insecurities

dear fathers of young women:
do not tell your daughters that their bodies
are only to be used for and by men
do not tell your daughters that their choices
about their bodies need approval from men
do not tell your daughters that they are any less
of a woman for doing something only for themselves

we decide
for our health
for our bodies
for our lives
for ourselves

BREAK FREE

there is nothing worse
than being trapped
within the prison cell
of abuse
sometimes
I put myself
into lockdown mode
alarms screaming
E M E R G E N C Y
* CODE RED *
get *OUT*
~~help me~~
break *f r e e*
escape
even in the dark
if I try to reach out
I still feel the cold bars
around me
always
a flicker of light
beyond them
always
further away

TIGER LILY

I'm the lone flower
in a field of weeds
looking towards the hopeful sun
fighting to survive
to be appreciated by none
only existing in this place
in beautiful, peaceful solitude
never to be picked from the earth
a rare beauty taken for granted
eventually to be withered and dead
never to be held
petals plucked for foolish wishes
instead I am
living to grow, to bloom, to survive
a full, blossoming life
of my own
on my own

MASKS

I am not afraid
of monsters

I am afraid
of the humans
they pretend
to be

take off your mask

CHAOS

without chaos
there would be no life
without life
there would be no beauty
without beauty
there would be no women
without women
there would be nothing

now reverse

HUNT

she is the red queen
wild wolves hunting for her heart
she will not give in

SPLINTERS

I am still teaching my bones
how not to crack
to shatter and collapse
under my own pressure
while repairing them
from his
do not touch me
if you are afraid
of a few splinters

work in progress, closed for repairs

CORPSES

I have always found enjoyment
in preserving the corpses
of the beautiful roses
he had given me
knowing when their lives
are slowly coming to an end
I have the power to flip fate
string them up by the stems
upside down and dry them out
hang a noose and leave untouched
in the same bouquet form
that brought their vibrancy to life
the scent of decaying roses
hallucinates and excites
I feel almost sadistic, selfish even
to prolong and imprison
every petal of their beauty
long after death has risen
so that I can reminisce through them
the memories of us I have left
kept alive, though I know
they are just as dead
as the faded red skeletons
lying next to my bed

there is beauty after death

FLAWS

once upon a time, I embraced my flaws
I will tell you about a few of them
open and honest

I have stretch marks on my skin
but I carried a child within
I have scars from head to toe
but I survived depression's low
I have curves for perfect grasping
but my body is not everlasting
I have cellulite on my thighs
but they are muscular in disguise
I have long hair less than it used to be
but an even thicker personality
I was born with a slight lazy eye
but I am damn happy to see and be alive
I have frequent panic attacks
but I stand up and snap right back
I have been broken by some men
but they will never touch me again
I have given into fear too freely
but it will never take away from me
I have been everything under the sun
but I came out brighter and I won
I have never fit in with other girls
but I realised this is a woman's world

and I have never
felt more beautiful

VIOLENT HEART

do not expect her
to be silent
her heart is on fire
and passionately
violent

IF THE COFFIN FITS

I was mourning you
while you were still living
breathing, walking
on this earth
I was prepared
to throw roses
into your grave
and wish you well
but you haunted me
buried me alive
pushing me into the dirt
at your own funeral

there's room for two

BREATHLESS

there is a fine line
between
breathless and suffocating
one is deadly
the other
exhilarating
how foolish are we
giving someone the chance
for both
to suffocate you
to take your breath away
perhaps
at the same time

isn't that what love does?

MY MAGIC

a perfect stranger
that believes in your magic
is more meaningful
than countless others
only believing in it
to steal for themselves
if you ask nicely
I have enough magic in me
to share with you too

LOVE TRAP

She did not tip-toe into love. No, instead she gripped
her heart that was bigger than her wide-open arms and
jumped in feet first. Hoping that if she drowned, her
heart would be large enough to keep her afloat. Her
legs were weighted by her own hopes, desires, beliefs,
and to her demise – foolishness.

She fell, she fell, she fell. Down a rabbit hole of rose
petals that felt like a dream come true. As she closed
her eyes, she let go of the heart that she was holding
onto so tightly for safety.

Only when she fell deep enough, she decided to open
her eyes. In an instant she landed amongst the thorns
of the countless others unable to escape and rise.
Trapped, she became another rose. Her petals lay
strewn into the abyss, welcoming and drawing in the
next.

don't use your heart as a life preserver

25

RED GOWN

his fingertips tore
jagged tears of blood
along every inch of her
he touched
try to heal her ravaged skin
bathe in thunderstorms, if she must
traces of beast stain her veil
a beast that lusts for Red
gave the gift of scars embellished
to decorate her dress instead
under the moon
she dances in the rain
white gown painted red
howling while the color bleeds
until she appears vibrant
instead of dead

Don't Touch Me

I would be lying
if I said I wasn't
terrified
to have another
whisper love
and touch me
even the word
feels like a knife
clawing at my skin
it makes
me want
to scream

the after effects

DEAR SLAVERY

oh, darling
how foolish of you
to believe
my loyalty
meant you gained
entitlement
ownership
property
of me

I am not caged
I belong to me
slavery
meet my bravery
as I set myself
free

RESCUE

you cannot breathe life
into someone
who enjoys suffocating
in their darkness

I've tried

SNAKES

why is it that
when we finally begin
to pursue our passions
achieve a spark of hope
find our smiles again
search for happiness
start *living* without them
snakes start to slither
out of the dark
to sink their venom
into any sweetness
we taste for ourselves

you are hissstory

EXPECTATIONS

if you expect someone
to be the light of your life
do not
do not
do not
drag them and dim them
into the darkness
of yours

our light is not to be taken for granted

FREEDOM FIRE

"Little Red, little Red, let me in."
cried the wolf in sheep's clothing.

"Not by the desires of my darkest sins."
replied a fierce Red.

"Then I'll huff, and I'll puff, and I'll destroy
everything you are."
he threatened.

"Try as you might, though last time you did not get
very far."
She smiled slyly, wrapping a cloak of fire around her
and setting herself aflame before flying off into the
night.

Alone and ashamed, the wolf howls mournfully at the
burning stars he calls Red. She lit up the sky every
night to remind him of the power he hungered for, but
could not take. Red danced around the moon until the
blazing sun called her home. Her freedom fire was a
striking display of beauty, strength, and grace. One to
remember forever.

the phoenix that got away

LANDMINES

my heart is a battlefield
my soul a veteran of war
tread lightly while you kiss my lips
brace for impact and explore
triggering landmines in my head

I am trying to surrender
remove shrapnel from my wounds
be cautious to approach me
a ticking time bomb perfumed

my heart is still a battlefield
my soul still at war with my mind
raise a white flag to myself
this battle is no-one's
but mine

IMBICILES

boys take for granted
the importance of women
as if they entered this world
immaculate gods among mortals

if they only knew the power it took
for their mothers to give the gift of life
to birth them through time portals
perhaps they would think twice
before disgracing her light

how truly terrible are those
who abuse their existence, their creation
claiming women as a prize for property
used for ego's pleasure – an abomination

if these imbiciles spent one day
seeing through our eyes
feeling our sacrifice
living our lives
I guarantee you
they would respect women right
although, most of the weakest
would likely not survive

WALK AWAY

monsters will try
to break you
drag you lower
than their hell
say and do things
to you, about you
unforgiveable
horrible
untrue
your strength lies
in walking away
rising above it
the only person
who can save you
is you
they are trapped
in their downward spiral
and you
deserve better

you deserve to live your life
instead of tangled in someone's chains

DEFIANT DEMISE

she drifted, falling – into the sound of silence
silence in scorched remnants of deafening violence
violence forced her cries toward his distant lies
lies hid screams of helpless defiance

had she not suffered enough by compliance
compliance felled upon her weaker alliance
alliance broken in shadow; innocent – she dies
she dies by the hands of man's dark subsidence

monster he is, master of cunning disguise
disguise that lived behind voided eyes
eyes can reveal reliance or guidance
guidance was his trickery unto her demise

SCORPIONS

I am convinced
scorpions live among us
not in the nightmares
you so fearfully dream up
or scurrying in the desert heat
but within human monsters
crawling and stinging
a pest that will not leave
never quite satisfied
just a nuisance
for the thrill of their ego
seeking out easy targets
projecting their natural state
of frantic, terrified rage
until someone
puts them out of their misery
cracks the shell of bravado
revealing the soft, black
abyssal mess
inside of them

I think I had one as a pet in another life
he probably stung himself to death and blamed me
R.I.P.

LET THEM GO

sometimes
you have to let people go
sometimes
love isn't enough
sometimes
the truth only sets you free
and when you do
you will love again
you will live again
better
without them

BURNING

the abyssal
love to obsess
over what they cannot have
dreams they lost
took for granted
never deserved
admiring her from afar
across bridges
they burned
hungry for a soul
destruction
no lessons learned
what do they expect
throwing kindling
into a fire
watch
as she emerges
into your envious
desires

she is a wildfire

WE WILL RISE

leave it to the man
who disgraces her
to proclaim
she fell from grace

darling, a goddess
does not fall
she rises
a phoenix
from her
ashen grave

*a woman's worth
is not determined by a man*

BATTERED

every door I have ever locked
has claw marks carved across it
blood and tears frantically painted
broken pins jammed into the keyholes
craters pelted into the surface
from trying to get back in

maybe
just maybe
they are meant to stay closed

and maybe
just maybe
the other side is just as damaged

NEXT

I have had
more goodbyes than hellos
more turned backs, masked faces
more silence than words
more shackles than freedom
so, please forgive me
for always fearing
what comes next

PAST TO POWER

to lock away the past
as if it were that simple
is to remove the parts of us
that we built our fortresses upon
that we forged our power from
that we carefully crafted
piece by piece
the magnificent work of art
that is a survivor

the past only exists within us
to force us to keep living
keep
building
keep
surviving

AGAIN

I will never allow myself
to be degraded again
if you are not helping me
to build my power
you don't deserve
to feel it

HONEY

he called me many things
that were not as sweet
as the day he called me *honey*
as if licking his lips
shaking his fists
raising his voice
meant that he loved me
it would be silly of me
to let him indulge
devour my sweet honey pot
but he is a bear
and he has claws
tempting
is it not

GENIE

"I will grant you any wishes,
your heart's desires,
only to be graced
by your smile's fire."
boasted the Genie,
grasping a burning trident.

"Peace."
I foolishly wished for.

and into the flames I went.

HER GARDEN

she finally realised
freedom tasted
sweeter than honey
letting go felt
empowering
healing was
disastrous

she was tired
of picking up her own pieces
watering dead plants

she buried the past
just like that
and planted her garden
on top of the soil

my god
did she live
and breathe
and *bloom*
beautifully
without him

CRITICS

if you spend your entire life
envious of what others achieve
you are going to be disappointed
for a very long time, my dear

if destroying people for your gain
helps you sleep at night
wake up and improve yourself
instead of seeking out their light

after all, the envious
are the biggest fans of the victorious

SNAP BACK

one day he will regret
not knowing how to love her
how bad it must have been
that the only option she had left
after trying so hard for nothing
was to walk away, screaming
from the only man
she wanted to love and be loved by
this is more than a breaking point
it is the brink of insanity
she knew that staying with him
meant to lose herself entirely
it felt like a fair enough trade
to rip out a part of her soul
and leave it with him
than to lose it all
if she stayed

sometimes I still feel him pulling on the strings
but I cannot snap back to him

DAMAGED GOODS

I do not want to be afraid
to fall in love again
considered damaged goods
after being broken and bent
or to hurt someone pure
with my sharpened blades
they need as much as I do
a love that saves
I am afraid of the past repeating
crawling out of the dark
ruining time left fleeting
I deserve to be happy
with a lifelong companion
though I can't help but believe
I am a love-cursed phantom

or maybe, that's what I was beaten into believing

Slow Down

I am never rushing again
not myself, not my life, not time
certainly not love

I am going to slowly savour
every lick of this lifetime
every taste upon my tongue
saving little crumbs if I can
labelled as memories in my mind

I will close my eyes
leave them open simultaneously
memorizing the feeling
of touching and being touched
fingers planting gardens and
claws digging deeper

I remember
the way my hair turns to icicles
my skin white as the snow
reflecting the sunrise
into my own pale pink sky
during an early morning winter freeze

I remember hands and eyes
just as cold and dark
as the long nights of December

I can remember the first snowfall
while melting under summer heat
swimming in the honey sweat
that drips from my chest
reminding me of the taste of yours

I can recall every detail
of my life that was not rushed
sometimes, I have to slow myself down
to remember your lips
on mine

Wings

am I supposed to fear
the quake beneath my feet
or begin dancing stronger
make it break a little longer
stomp it – smash it
crush it – outlast it
until the ground gives in
below me

am I supposed to fear
the chaos life brings

no

my secret is
I have wings

DEATH OF ME

you'll be the death of me
she said, living for him
until she decided
to live for herself
instead

and it was a life worth living

FROZEN

we were winter lovers
hearts as cold as the night
set on fire by furious shivers
our bodies colliding into inferno
melting the snow around us
a chilling grave fit for both
kisses that froze our lips together
agony as we ripped them apart
left to taste a tortuous memory
within icicles of our blood
as snowflakes disappeared
on our tongues
on our flesh
we burned into each other
melted away with them
our season departed
as did we
until the first
snowfall
begins

LIMITS

I refuse to entertain
an insecure man
projecting and blaming
his faults whenever he can
onto a faithful woman
who has always been honest
and subjected herself
to his destruction and mispromise
I refuse to believe in a man
who trusts his obscurity
instead of the truth, he chooses
jealousy beyond mortality
I cannot help a man
who enjoys swimming in the dark
never trying to find the light
he shields his eyes from it
before it sparks
I do not have to stay
with a man who ignores
walks away from a woman
who he knows he does not deserve
or the love she gives him every day
I will not waste my life waiting
on a boy who cannot mature
every woman has her limits
she will have enough
and walk out of the door

KEEP CLIMBING

I will tremble and quake
I will fall
I have broken and crumbled
I have crawled
I am built upon pieces
of these tragic releases
and I
will climb
above all

THE QUEEN

a queen forged in fire
dancing in his flames
for so long
are you surprised
she rises a phoenix
burning all
who have done her
wrong

THE KING

demons took one moment
to show their darkness to me
nothing compared
to the prolonged torment
the devil was gifting for free
a million chances to lash again
every opportunity was taken
flaming stakes into my flesh
falling into love forsaken
try to escape, I lose my path
demons dragging me
endlessly
to the king of hell
and back

TREMBLE

her bloody lips
could seize
the devil's black heart
collapsing him
on his knees
begging
~~for a taste~~
to tear them apart

DIFFERENCES

the difference
between him
and me

he suffocated everything
and I needed
to breathe

he turned light into dark
and I needed
to see

he was a cage
and I needed
to be free

two different pieces in the wrong puzzle

ONE LOVE

you will have one love in your life
one that smells like sunshine
when frost numbs your fingertips
and tastes like honey
while licking the thorns of roses
one love like a hurricane
sweeping you off your feet
spinning you dizzy
crashing you back into yourself
a love that is beautiful
destructive yet tragic
one love that you long for
wish for by magic
though just like the storm it brings
it passes too

goodbye, Hurricane Blue

TEMPTATION

but I do love him
said Red, about the wolf man
I'm a fool for claws

how can I resist
with teeth equally as sharp
wolf man, ravage me

CHILLS

as wind slips
through spaces
between
my fingers

I'm reminded
by the shivers

so do you

BAD HABIT

I used to think
my smoking addiction
would kill me quicker
but you
oh, you burned me out faster
than an after-sex cigarette
left me smouldering
drained of life
ashes upon the sheets
you
would be the death of me
a bad habit
I will spend the rest
of my days and nights
recovering from

HAUNTED HEART

a woman's heart
is like a haunted house
the most terrifying you will ever see
sheltering ghosts and demons of the past
unable to be released

unexpected fears and nightmares
around every corner she explores
her windows and doors are sealed
boarded shut with heavy remorse

the dark is seldom pierced
shards of light through fading cracks
that will illuminate the horrors of her
a sheltered beauty hidden in the back

she tries to keep out the monsters
that live within her, screaming instead
do not enter or be forever trapped
for the haunted house of her heart
is but only an entrance
to the many rooms inside her head

beware room 143

PERMISSION

this may come as a shock
to some men
but us women
we are allowed to leave you
we are allowed to walk away
we are allowed to escape
we are allowed to say no
no matter how much
we love you
no matter how many times
we forgive you
no matter how many chances
we provide you
if we are continually
beaten down
ignored and disrespected
abused and taken for granted
degraded into nothing
you best prepare yourself
to be left with exactly that
when she has enough
and walks away
leaving you with
nothing

WINE DRUNK

I loved you
until the last sip of my sanity
alas, like the death I swallowed
to drown the nightmares of you
to help me sleep at night
to forget you
I soon realised you were emptier
than the cold bottle in my hands
and even more toxic to me
than the poison in my veins

letting go never tasted so good

My Addiction

I swallowed every word of his
spat out with a flowered tongue
serpents wrapped carefully
hidden around a loaded gun

like a leech seeking sustenance, I believed them
drinking poison, drowning in him foolishly dazed
until I became devoid of life
heavy doses sparked fatality in a haze

left frantic to have one last fix
before I set myself free
I did not want to admit he was bad for me
I enjoyed the high hopes in his flattery
too much, I was addicted to the fantasy
of what could be, should be, wouldn't be

he knew my soul was hopelessly ethereal
so far from planes of this reality
I had to wake myself out of it
my dream, turned nightmare – now tragedy

I realised in time, if I could save my mind
before my blood ran cold
eyes would stay closed
never

though injecting his empty promises
trying to keep myself alive
would have been the death of me
forever

I Am Not Sorry

~~I apologise~~
     no, I don't
~~I am sorry~~
     no, I'm not

I am proud of myself
to have come this far
to be confident enough
to dry my own tears

I am not sorry
for coming on too strong
it took me long enough
to get here

I am not sorry
for using my voice
I have been silent
for too many years

I am proud of myself
for the woman I am
the woman I was
and the woman
that has yet to appear

You Knew

you said it yourself
that I deserve better
still knowing that
you did not
even
try

when you are alone
blaming me
for leaving
you only need
ask yourself
why

MASTER OF DISASTER

give me your disasters
I will shape and form them
into a sculpture of beauty
future's empire enfolded

give me your thunderstorms
I will show you that lightning
can spark a fire between us
passion's hurricane igniting

give me your chaos
I will bring you to your knees
to show you that none of this
has any power over me

I am not afraid of being destroyed
for I too have caused destruction
there is nothing to compare or calm
a scorned woman's volcanic eruption

PENGUINS

like penguins do
you made a nest of stones
and somehow
I felt
comfortable

they also steal from other penguins to build them
appearing to have done all the hard work themselves

a bed built on betrayal and dishonesty
is not a bed to sleep peacefully in

FREEDOM

is loving yourself
belonging to no one
finding happiness
in everything you do

freedom is a child's laughter
and living in the moment
making every second count

life is too short to be unhappy
unloved
and broken down

take a deep breath
wake up with the sun
run away

and be free

UNPREDICTABLE

today is one of those days
that I can relate to the most
patches of heavy rainfall
probably a rainbow
somewhere
blue skies to my left
storm clouds to my right
the sun playing
hide and seek
leaves falling
by the hundreds
a strong wind
suddenly quiet
like always
I am left wondering
with my own emotions
what on earth
will happen next

ENIGMA

there is a certain enigma about him
I can't quite place my finger upon
captivating me inch by inch
so, I will use my lips instead
try to whisper sense to myself
fail horribly, I grasp for his hands
giving into delightful mystery
with my imaginary gentleman

*When you've been without a love for a while, you
begin to dream it into existence to make sense of the
longing – or, at least I do – somewhere between what
was real, and what I wished was real.*

*I suppose a perk of having a wild imagination is you're
never really lonely. Dream/write up a lover –
sometimes, they'll treat you better than reality has.*

TREMORS

do you ever
have that feeling
laying very still
in the center of your bed
eyes closed shut
slow breathing
quiet
and it feels like
an earthquake
is shaking it and you
but you realise
it is only the rhythm
of your heart beating
powerfully

the same thing happens
when I think of you
except those earthquakes
are very real
collapsing me
to my core

CHAOTIC CREATION

I am not a stable
person, lover, woman
I am very much an earthquake
and I ache to quake
wreaking havoc so maniacally
it is visible from space
I love to roll in the ruins
of myself and you
and I love
to tear down empires
marvelling at what I can do
my foundation is shaky
crumbling beneath me
yet magically
I piece everything
back together
intricately
so much better
after every disaster
I thrive
in the wake of chaos
it feeds my creation
and I wait patiently, anxiously
for the tremors to return

LETTERS TO HIM

there were many letters written to him
damage exerted, screaming by pen
I immortalised his memories
in the ink from my heart that bled

I kept these messages from my soul
between the blurry lines of my poems
in hopes they might have reached him
if he ever doubted or felt alone

nothing was really left unsaid
I raised my voice enough to be heard
to say love never existed between us
would be a false statement absurd

but life changes people, people are only mortals
distance causes rifts, time opens portals

though destruction was caused
pieces broken, pages torn
I can say with confidence that I loved
I fought, and stayed until I could no more

I believe souls connect for a reason
lessons were learned in our changing seasons

I forgive you in my fragile healing
the strength it takes to let you go
howling at the full moon still
mourning you through my window

DOES FOREVER EXIST?

I can't remember
the last time I touched
tasted, felt – kissed
forever
that strange instant
time stops, life rushes
around us
when I close my eyes
a faint, delightful peace
lingering for a moment
on and under my skin
that feeling, I would describe
in one word – as forever
but forever does not exist
as our bodies and lips sever
eyes open, arms let go
of together
I fear holding
forever
again
never

was it real?

maybe forever exists between souls
certainly not in the physical

CONTRADICTION

I am selflessly selfish
if that makes any sense
I mean no misunderstanding
or taken offense
if I'm brutally honest
I will help you off a fence
but you are likely
to land on my side
a walking contradiction
I am myself
I will gladly help others
expecting nothing from them
only my own satisfaction
sitting polished on a shelf
a perfectionist in details
I will correct your mistakes
to help you flourish while
keeping my pride in place
it's a win-win really
you get what you want and so do I
very much like a rainbow
kisses storming skies
ironic balance creates
compromise

SIGNS

signs given to us
by universal screams
a message
keep going
ignore them and it will grow louder
sometimes we can guess
what each one means
a guide along the path
of life
reminders to keep our light
do not lose your fight
keep going
though these calls may
happen simultaneously
to another
it does not always mean
go back that way
to each other
it could simply mean
keep going

you're on the right path

PARADOX

losing someone
I never knew to begin with
feels beyond proud disappointment

proud that I dreamed up a real love
imagining a perfect starlit night
a tall, dark, mysterious man
I never did see his face though
but I would recognise his presence
if our paths crossed again

disappointed that I will never have him
because he does not exist
the feelings I have are real of course
perhaps from another lifetime
where I knew him, and I saw his eyes
maybe I would recognise him in yours

I awake and he disappears
left grieving in my consciousness
until I fall asleep again, reunited at last

I do this to myself constantly
trapped in a land
between dream and reality
with my paradoxical mystery man

SILENT SCREAMS

I faintly recall
the sound of your voice – my name
buried beneath silent screams

my screams... or yours?
trapped within confusion – don't
they still haunt my dreams

when night is silent
a ringing in my ears – stop
I don't want to hear

CORE OF LONGING

longing for him tortures
I need him in my core
from the very moment
he pulls himself away
I want more
from my body – escaping
in a moment of ecstasy
perfect bliss, I scream
come back to me
he plants the sweetest part
of him deep inside of me
always I will want more
I anticipate to absorb
please leave me full
like a patient moon waiting
this desire is insatiable
his for the taking
I crave his magic
exploding
into me

A Slow Death

loving you in silence
is akin to slowly dying
but alas, in the end
we are all silent
when we die
maybe this
is our
eternity
after all

You Will Heal

endings are painful
moving on is terrifying
grieving is a nightmare
count your stars
hold onto the good
of the past, present, and future
it will patch your wounds
remind you to smile and
you will heal
you will heal
you will heal

ILLUSIONS

I never cared too much
for illusions
always predictable
easy to dissect
I don't care too much
for illusive mortals either
always predictable
easy to dissect
give me yourself raw
one look in the eyes
that's all I need
to break your disguise

I've got you figured out

HEARTS OF CHILDREN

how truly beautiful it is
that our children's hearts beat
from the same rhythm
ours echo into theirs
as women
we are the only beings
to carry two hearts
two souls
within our bodies
at once
how miraculous
and magical
it is
to be a mother

and to carry my own heart outside of my body

WOMEN ON FIRE

you are a force truly
to be reckoned with
the holiest of unholy hellfire
do you even realise
what you are capable of
who you are, who you have been
who you are about to become
the sheer enormity of the power
you hold just crackling within
your spitfire eyes and devilish lips
shooting magic from your fingertips
do not ever doubt your worth
before a volcano erupts
she sleeps quietly first
you are a woman and you shall roar
never let silence be a winning force
I will roar with you
we will rise together
spark fires with the stars of night
exploding, burning into forever
and they, the ones who told us
we were and would be
nothing
will become speechless instead
as they look at us now
us women on fire
oh, goddess
we are something

I DREAM IN PURPLE

I dream in a world of purple
where skies are painted of lavender
oceans marooned with depth
my forests bloom thickets of plum
iris-kissed lips with exhaled breath
the sunlight glistens at dawn for me
through a haze of violet light
a full moon and clouds of orchids
comfort me in the sleepless night
everything around me is amethyst
a combination of tragic and lush
beauty in the stars that fall on me
periwinkle eyes cry indigo hushed
my lilac soul creates new shades
of purple
upon everywhere
I touch

within this world
I live an artist's dream
right here
I am enough

OVERWHELMED

she begged to feel nothing
she pleaded to feel something
she began to feel everything
it was all too much
at once

WOLF CRY

she is a wolf at heart
the only cry
she howls
is a call for freedom
into the dark
one she had to answer
alone
hunting
for herself

FRAYED KNOTS

love should not be an excuse
to imprison yourself to abuse
rather, a dignified reason
to escape it
and untangle yourself
from his noose

use the rope to free yourself and climb out

EVE

oh, delightful good man
of heavenly god's taste
I detect you are becoming vexed
I wonder, if your robes of white
could use a splash of red
have you repented, begged mercy
for all of your sins forgiven
shrouded beneath your halo I see
give in
give in
I know what you are hiding
secret sinner of mine
let your demons out to play
in the eve of serpent's vine
how long since you felt passion
does it ache within your bones
surrender to temptation
free your priestly woes
if to love fiercely
is to commit sin
crucify me now
give in
give in
to me

UTOPIA

words have the power
to create or destroy
emerging from magicians or fools
razor-sharp tongues of the spiteful
can whisper a darkness so cruel
snakes enjoy the endless torment
seeping venom under skin to flow
believers of creation cannot be harmed
using their power and choosing to grow
turning nightmares into dreamscapes
living by magic of their utopic world
nothing can burn the fearless woman
who survived the abyss unfurled

Too Late

one day she will find
a love that she deserves
a lover deserving of hers
for better and for worse
and it will be too late
when you finally realise
you lost her

Too Much

too many chances
too many dances
not
enough
love
never again

too much forgiveness
taken as permission
for him to destroy her
once again

DESSERT

I would give into him
yes, in a heartbeat
if only mine was still beating
you see, a price is paid
when you sin with the devil
an appetizer – my heart
from his hands he was eating
he said, "it tastes delicious
a rare beauty you are, my dear
irresistible and half-alive"
licked his lips and with a smile
laid me lifelessly
upon his bed of knives
elegant and bloody
beautiful as all hell's fire
oh, you should have seen me
in my wedded attire
as he waited patiently
to devour my life
he enjoyed with pleasure
watching his main course
in his arms
slowly
fade
die

he preferred his women rare

CIRCUS FREAK

I was the star of the show
not my own – but his
forced to leap through fire hoops
scarring permanence onto my skin
balancing his fragile tightrope
lest I fall upon a bed of knives
flip over at his demand
or be lashed a thousand times
when you cage a wild woman
do not be surprised
when she bites back
and devours
your circus of lies

and you become more than circumcised

ICARUS

craft your wings
carefully
with gilded feathers
magnificently
now light them up
defiantly
let yourself soar
fearlessly

don't be afraid of flying into the sun
you are more powerful than the sun

LOVE YOURSELF

why would loving yourself
ever be considered selfish
there is more than enough
room in our hearts
for many people we love
for many types of love
including our own
this is the only body we have
the only experience we have
in this lifetime
it would be foolish
not to love it
nurture it
be proud of it
you deserve
to love yourself first

When you truly love yourself, you build a foundation for a safe home in your heart to shelter love for others. The love inside you grows stories higher. Love yourself first, and don't ever feel guilty for doing what is best for you and your foundation. The residents who stay in your heart will thank you, and help you patch up any tears.

TRANSFUSION

darling, you are not
and never will be
the blood in my veins
that keeps me alive
I transfused you
of that privilege
ages ago
it is no miracle
I still survived

I can live without your poison

Hang In There

the greatest epiphany
one can have
is learning
to embrace the good
despite the bad
realising that everything
happens for a reason
and people will change
just like the seasons
if you can conquer
and train your mind
to be open and accept
the wonders you find
you will notice
not everything
is what it seems
look beyond
venture for peace
it exists not only
in your dreams
but in every moment
in you, in me
if you can be patient
and remain strong
through all adversity
you will see
every chaos
has a calm

STRANGER

I stopped missing you
when I realised
the person I loved
ceased to exist
a long time ago
and missing a stranger
did not make much sense
to me

who are you?

RISE AND FALL

why are we always falling?
falling in love
stumbling on our feet
collapsing in fear
spiralling downward
why do we not move up?
and rise, float
ascend
fly into love
dance on our feet
balance, balance, balance
gravity, gravity
excuses
why can't we
prevent ourselves
from falling
over
under
down

without falling first
we would never learn how to rise

GROWTH

yes
my darling
the dirt is dark
rooted with the past
but look
my darling
at the beauty
and new life
that grows
and blooms
from it

grow your own garden, my darling

*When you feel like dirt, close your eyes, and imagine
flowers growing from the deepest parts of you.
Feel their colours. You know what waters them?
Love. Hope. You.*

I DON'T

I am slowly accepting
my wedding will happen
only in my dreams
at night I close my eyes
a bridge of rose petals
appears in front of me
I smile, take a step forward
I see him smiling too
then everything turns dark
after I say – I do
falling back to reality
eyes open, a tearful stream
fragments of hope still lingering
while I silence a cosmic scream

FIREFLIES

she took the darkest parts of herself
held tightly in enclosed hands
and lit them up like

fireflies

TOUGH LOVE

I never learned anything
in life
about life
by the hands of
gentle lessons
in order to carve
a sculpture
out of stone
you need to use
precision cuts
brute force
to shape it into
a masterpiece

a lesson
the artist
and the creation
both understand
in the end

NOURISH

water my soul
with the magic of you
a petal's touch
will never do

REMEMBER ME

when I die
my mind will fade
a final wish released
I hope my soul
continues to write
I hope some corners
are creased
I hope you carry me
with you
across the pages
of your memories
there
I will live
forever
safe and resting
at peace

THUNDERSTORMS

thunder does not scare me
nor does lightning in the night
the flashes are strikingly beautiful
unpredictable partners
of thunder's might
a downpour of electric droplets
crashes onto the earth below
I am aching to dance with them
as the storm within me grows

DREAMS

I have so many dreams
I wish to bring to life
both within myself
and in my daughter's eyes

SNOWFALL

I will fall for you
like the softness of snow
exciting you at the first sight
blanketing you in my beauty
turning barren trees
into a wonderland
where you stand
the first snowfall
is only the beginning
before I become a blizzard
freezing your heart
your bones will begin
aching into your core
until you shiver
at the thought of me
running inside
for warmth

you won't find it

SACRIFICE

it takes a lot
to make me scared
since becoming a mother
I realised very fast
nothing could terrify me more
than her own pain
if I could chase away
all of her nightmares
if I could cry
every tear for her
if I could relieve all of her fears
to give her infinite peace
take every insecurity away
as my own
I would do so
in the same heartbeat
we share
my last breath
would be for her
if I could
I would do it all
for her
just to see her
smile

WE LEARN

I started writing
at a very young age
but I was taught
journals and diaries
are to be kept secret
by little girls

but little girls grow up
learning to teach
themselves
and now
I am sharing my story
with the world

we grow
we learn
we flourish

EPHEMERAL

love is everlasting
unconditional and transcendent
the physical ties we bind by
are ephemeral and fleeting
beyond unexpected endings
love still remains after we part
it is a connection never torn
etched in our souls and our hearts
though hands may release
from each beloved grasp
we are still one
in future and past
distance may cause rifts
our love still exists
eternal in us
the physical
is short-lived

EQUALS

I am a woman
I have loved men
I have loved women
one thing is certain
women know
what women want
men know
what men want
only a real love
understands both
for both
regardless of difference
yet respectful of it
that, my darling
is rare

*Both are equally capable of loving you, and destroying
you just the same. Find the one who holds your heart
like it is the center of the universe, and would never be
the cause of its collapse.*

FIRE FOOD

he came into my life
like a whirlwind of fire
before I knew it
I was carried away
burning into his embers
a pretty casualty
along his path
of destruction
that only fed
his flames

THREE'S A CROWD

oh, he will have his threesome
though not with me involved
instead, with what he hates
and loves the most
his ego, karma, and himself

just wait until pride shows up
you're in for a treat

CHINA

oh, please do – I beg
shatter me like glass
step on my remains
free me at last
I would love
to get under your skin
retaliate my pain
break me open fast
let me breathe again
yet I know
you would avoid me still
walk past me, even broken
china in a cabinet
locked away
your fragile token

SKIES OF WINTER

skies of winter remind me
cold approaches, bleak and grey
a blanket of snow envelops the earth
identical – my pale skin on display
bitter chills will tickle my bones
tempted – disguise an angel in play
even the elements know that I am not
I dive in, we melt away
the skies of winter remind me
nothing warm can stay

BALLOONS

fill up balloons
with the dust inside my lungs
let them rise
carry worry away

each balloon for a wish
a dream that was missed
like the countless kisses
that never
stood a chance

float away, my balloons
I am breathing new air in
it is so much sweeter than old

goodbye my balloons
until the last that remains
is a weighted dream colored
in gold

up

up

up   *and stay*

FORGIVE HER

a woman carried wild in her heart
her soul abstract painted – a fine art
eyes commanded full attention
a gathering of nature's companions
singing songs of mischief dancing
untamed freedom, forest prancing
wildflowers tucked in hair she picked
ruled tiny kingdoms made of sticks
dreamer and lover by moonlit magic
she met a fate by a man so tragic
forced into cages – had she sinned?
forgive her for the freedom
she so lived

BORROWED TIME

time
does not
deplete love – no
it amplifies over fleeting
moments
we realise
can be lost
by closing of eyes
instantly
and slowly
slipping through fingers
hold onto every memory
cherish
every second
with loved souls
we live on borrowed
time

ENSLAVED TO LOVE

I loved and I loved, until there was none left to love
or surely this fate would be the death of me
I stayed and I stayed, until comfort was only dreamt of
I loved and I loved, until there was none left to love
depleted of my forces – hopeless silence from above
regardless of this twisted cage, I would set myself free
I loved and I loved, until there was none left to love
or surely this fate would be the death of me

THE NEVER LOVES

I have had enough of the never loves
the could not be, should not be
would not be loves
the will not, the cannot
do not know loves
the hate loves, the hurt loves
e m p t y loves

I am longing of the capable loves
the genuine, the honest
respectful loves
the comforting, the trusting
unconditional loves
the real loves, the rare loves
happy loves

the healthy love
that my soul requires
to be free and grow

I cannot, and will not
love from inside a cage
I deserve sunlight
a love
without decay

GLITTER

cover me in glitter
let my body place stars
upon your lips
lift each delicate sparkle
with your sticky honey kiss
and feel
me
d
r
i
p

MASTER

allow me to indulge, sir
beckon me to my knees
please
do not underestimate
the power of my tease

watch me dance flames around you
an inferno of tempting taste
dominate by my luscious name
desire entices burning haste

touch me with demanding eyes
slowly salivating – mesmerized
savour pale flesh and feed me fire
unity in soul's connection is revived

sin with me into salacious heaven
consume and command – I obey
lend me ascension by lethal injection
into my master's arms – I stay

TIMEKEEPER

wasting time
and time wasted
have two different meanings
time that is gone forever
and time that is still
remaining

use it wisely

INTUITION

my intuition has always been
the sharpest tool in my armoury
also, the most overlooked
taken for granted weapon
of my own mass destruction
and my saving grace
a life preserver
if only I had been smart enough
to pull on its strings
when the tide came in
or jumping from an airplane
never using the parachute
resting silently on my back
my entire being screams "don't"
but to my own demise, I do
ignoring my intuition
meant risking my life
sometimes
I liked living
in danger
sometimes
I was danger
jumping
from my own cliffs

ARTEMIS

take me to trek through the wilderness of your soul
I ache to grasp my fingers around your elements
together we roam ravenous for an insatiable hunt
embrace the adventure, for I am your Artemis

petrichor seeps into our sanguine veins
sweet dewy exhales birth pines of wildlife
skyward to the moon sacred intensity rises
animals bow in worship – creation ignites

a goddess of the quest I will seek out your heart
the highest treasured of humanity's all
in every burn of your ravaged, blessed blood
you will be possessed into heeding my wild call

WARRIOR WOMAN

a stampede of stallions
rushes through her heart
pounding like a drum
she stands tall and screams
for she is *she*
a woman
conquering free
fighting for all she loves
she rises
living for all she believes
fear the wild within her eyes
warrior woman
she is *me*

ENOUGH

she said
enough
and
just like that
she was
it was
all was
enough

just like that

CUT THEM OFF

cut off a narcissist's supply
and watch how frantic
they become
the masks they held in place
will quickly come undone
revealing to the world
their true colors on their own
a void of control
lacking in themselves alone
they suffocate in their suffering
attention is a lifelong craving
cut off their obsession quickly
or you will lose yourself in saving

QUILTED MAN

I wish I had kept more reminders
somehow collected enough pieces
to fabricate
a fragmented, quilted version of you
within my dream-state reality
in a way I do
often pricking my fingertips
with imaginary needles
stitch by stitch into a masterpiece
picking and choosing my favorite
memories and feelings of everything
sewing them into the best version of you
I can make with my mind's hands
every pattern and color I fell in love with
in my mismatched quilted man
sometimes the stuffing falls out
corners fade and threads fray
but it's all made up of the pieces
that I have left of you
the parts that remain
holding the good above all
I arrange them together every day
if this is all I have left of you
I wouldn't have it any other way

HER HAND

she is a goddess
more than you could
ever understand
that's where you made
your first mistake
to claim her
she knows her worth
beginning to end
and you
do not deserve
her hand

WOLF DANCERS

if you ever find me lost
wandering blind beneath the stars
follow my cosmic howl for you
under the same moon, never apart

a moonlit path to walk with you
side by side on a silent night
feel the magic inside of us
become full with the moon tonight

if you ever find yourself lost
wandering blind beneath the stars
I will find you here as we begin
a dance of wolves in the dark

GUILTY PLEASURES

I am guilty
of a multitude of pleasures
none such as delightful
as ruffling a few feathers

I adore arising storms
more often than not
basking in my destruction
secretly hoping to be caught

a maniacal laugh I do erupt
when my onslaught of trouble
shatters your dainty barriers
wreaking havoc to fragile bubbles

I am guilty of enjoying
the punishment that comes after
call me crazy if you will, but
I make love to the brink of disaster

TOGETHER

together
or apart
hold me gently
in your heart – safe
forever

together
we can
drown the desert
create an oasis of
love

together
we create
a better way
of learning how to
understand

together
we live
together we die
all living – all are
dying

together
no more
never doubt yourself
you are entirely whole
already

HERBACEOUS

she is a witch of an herbal magic
planting gardens in the soil of her past
she chooses each fern and flower
knowing secretly which ones will last
if she feels like her memory
is slipping through her fingers
pluck a sprig of déjà vu
steep tea and she remembers
some of her plants bloom by season
but her belladonna – shadow hidden
she keeps alive
for a deadly reason

contemplating herbicide

142

RETREAT

for now
I will lock myself away
into my own tower
built brick by brick
by raw trembling hands
guarded by no beast
only the ferocity
of my own heart
for now
I will retreat
to find my solace again
where my dreams
bleed into reality
peaceful solitude
pleasant solidarity
for now
I heal
for now
I let go
for now
I rescue myself

GENTLE GIANT

I will have a gentle giant
with gentle hands
and gentle voice
a true gentleman
his gentle words
from gentle lips
gentle eyes closing
before gentle kiss
gentle footsteps
lead gentle glide
and for once
I will sleep
gently
by his gentle side

PETALS

love me until I wither
water me until I bloom
shine your sunlight
into my veins
please don't
pluck my petals
too soon

TEST ME

scream at me
one more time
I'll show you
my silence
overpowers you

disrespect me
one more time
I'll show you
I respect myself
without you

raise your fists
one more time
I'll show you
how I raise mountains
around you

lose your chances
one more time
I'll show you
I am never giving another
to you

CLIMATE CHANGE

I am the frost that sets in around you
the coldest winter you have ever felt
a trembling, shaking within you
begging for the ice to melt

I am the wind that suffocates
an overdose of oxygen released
to steal the breath from your lungs
leave you gasping, crawling on your knees

I am the oasis and the desert heat
scorching you with quenching thirst
a haze overpowering senseless lust
you decide which comes first

I am also the fire that ignites you
burning you from the inside all over
if you don't believe in climate change
fall in love with me, I'll show you
a natural disaster
from which you will never recover

DESERVING

if you are jealous
throwing accusations
of imaginary men, who might
give her the love she needs
would treat her right
ask yourself
why that man is not you
how you failed her, lost her
proving promises untrue
you know she deserves
better than this
let her be happy
find true love's kiss
save her the nightmares
let her be free
she deserves love
even if only in her dreams

a spiteful man is one
who knows she deserves better
but will never try to be a better man

PERFECT

his idea of a perfect woman
is one who never leaves
forgive me, but
I am not a slave to love
bound by chains
around my knees
try to hold me captive
you are damn right
I will stand and leave
I am perfect without him
stop your begging and revenge
please
I am not coming back
ever
I saved myself
from his chains
released

don't allow yourself to be broken down
to fit inside his cage
break the chains instead
you are perfect without him

I WILL LIVE

I survived before him
I will survive after him
any man who thinks
I do not have the power
to live without him
never deserved
to feel my power
with him

ONE DAY

one day her dreams will
become flowers in a bouquet
floating along a white aisle
instead of decaying
in her grave

one day

ALL IS HEALING

healing
healing
all of this
is healing
from that which
destroys us
from those who
have tried

LISTEN TO HER

while he ignores her
someone is wishing
to listen

she will
be heard

she will
be found

she will
be invisible
no more

you are not invisible
I see you, I hear you, I will listen

LABELS

you may foolishly
label me insensitive
I am so much worse

I create chaos
as much as I can seize it
feelings are a curse

madness is my muse
I draw it out like bloodwork
twisted mind's rebirth

watch what happens next
from the flames arise beauty
magic-maker, first

WHO TOLD YOU

who carved it into your soul
that you must break
before you become whole
who told you to shred your being
rearrange the pieces
into someone worth seeing
who disgraced the stars in your eyes
scattered across darkness
until you realised
the bigger picture of who you are
who told you
you were not born complete
that you must be torn down
forced to admit defeat
to unleash the fire within you
to burn who you are
to ignite yourself again
to rise from your own ashes
you are born of those stars
you have always been
burning
do not be destroyed
by another, instead
tell yourself
I am learning

sometimes we need to self-destruct
to become a phoenix

REBUILD

I used to think falling in love
was the hard part – it's not
falling in love is innocent and easy
it's falling out of love
and walking away
that will shred you apart
and make you rebuild yourself

while you're still

c
  r
u
  m
b
  l
i
  n
g

BREATH OF LIFE

I wonder
where the life goes
that escapes my lungs
each breath
that used to be
a part of me
now something more
a part of you
my life
a part of all
that lives and breathes
that soars and falls
we are living
and dying
together

until the earth
gives her last exhale

the earth, she breathes
we inhale her life, yet exhale her death
how terribly tragic, that we take each breath
for granted

Wishes

I started running out
of things to wish upon
I never saw a shooting star in the sky
four leaf clovers were elusive as leprechauns
rainbows had no beginning or end
birthday candles tried to burn me
dandelion seeds blew back into my face
so, I started to pluck
at my own petals
instead
hoping one day
if I made a wish on myself
enough times
maybe
just maybe
I could make them
come true

I ran out of petals too

INTIMIDATE

does it scare you
a woman
who knows her worth
who uses her voice
demands respect first
does she scare you
or are you scared
because you don't
in the slightest
scare her

DANCE FOR HIM

dance for me
he said to her
the only spotlight
his demanding eyes

play me your favorite song
she said to him
her lips curled
into an innocent smile

he made her
scream for him
instead

he was the only one dancing too

Poisonous

I am not as delicate as you think
my poison packs a punch
sweet nectar makes you weak

You Don't Scare Me

I threw caution to the breeze
and it slapped me back
in the face repeatedly
wake up lady
read the warning signs
stop ignoring the alarms
listen to your intuition
count the red flags
that all built up a man
who I knew would destroy me
what on earth was I thinking
kissing him made even the skies
scream in fear and erupt
the wind told me to run with it
I planted my feet deeper
stared into his dark eyes
and said
do your worst
I'll show you
what I'm made of too

I was built to survive storms

PLAY WITH FIRE

I heard you enjoy
the bad girls – playing with fire
how about these ones

the women – on fire
do you think we swallow flames?
oh, yes we ignite

we consume your heat
dancing in a blaze of lust
we become wildfires

if you're afraid of the heat, stay out of my sheets

LIFELINE

the more I gave into him
the more I lost myself
and I was addicted
trapped in a cycle
believing what he gave me
in return
was enough
to keep me alive

it wasn't

TIMID

she had enough
of the cage he had carefully
constructed around her
with his bare hands
took the time to hammer
another bar of iron into it
every time her back was turned
she was tired
of being mistreated
as a pet
too afraid
to look up
when he said
her name

DEAR ME

Look at how far you've come. How many challenges you've faced, how many battles you've won. Marvel at yourself, you came out burning brighter than the sun. People who tried to pull you down put themselves beneath you instead. You are standing tall with beauty and a crown upon your head. You are raising a little girl from your own arms since the first moment she opened her eyes and saw you. She shared her first breath with your air and inherited your strength by the blood of your beating heart. You have every reason to never give up hope. Never stop believing in magic, no matter what comes or how tragic. I believe in you. Look at how far you've come. Life has only just begun.

Disenchanting

heed no exaggeration
disenchantment is upon us
I fear the world
is losing faith in magic
pompous tyrants carve hate
into hearts of children
women, men – heartbreakingly tragic
I am dreading the future
for our children, their children
generations to come
a world without magic
is a world without love
a woven miracle
will soon come undone

don't stop believing in magic
the world depends on it

DANGER

the anger that rises inside of him
when I tell him
you cannot touch me
you cannot have me
I am not yours
I never will be
no
stop
go away
and he ignores me
does it anyways
is exactly how I know
he is dangerous
it is exactly why
I left

among other reasons

Sweet Nothings

whisper to me
your sweet nothings
and I will give you
something
to scream about

a promise, and a threat

THE BIRDS

she awoke to an aviary chorus
singing softly in her ears
open eyes to strange places
surely, she had not been here
sunlight she felt beneath her skin
though she could not tell
what season earth was in
a singsong of sparrows
black crows erupt, louder
a strange cacophony indeed
something stranger – about her

trapped within nightmarish dream
a swarm of birds inside her
oh, they began to scream!
freedom! they caw – freedom at last!
as they peck and they pluck
her caged skin painfully fast
a dark cloud of black wings
circles ominously above her head
swooping in for the kill
the symphony of her past
she so dreads

RUINED

would you understand me
would you love me better
if I painted my heart
a little bit darker than this
if I mixed in a drop of poison
some shadows here and there
to mimic your growing abyss
slightly jagged brush strokes
a cigarette burn, maybe pin pokes
why not toss aside this gentle brush
a sharper tool would suffice very much
how about this, do you like it
are you proud, does it matter
my heart matches yours now
blackened and battered

MY MASKS

the masks I wear
are not masks at all
I am hiding no monster
I reveal myself on call
rather, a change in emotion
a flash of personality
it all depends on people
the environment around me
one of these you should fear
when I put on my goddess face
she brings hell's upheaval around her
puts you brutally back in your place
a smirk of mischievous madness
maniacal happiness by chance
a chameleon of change only
with whom I choose to dance
the masks I wear
are not masks at all
they are parts of me
my highest rises
and darker falls

DRAG ME

drag me back screaming
across acres I burned
between you and me
have I not learned yet
this lust for your flames
craves agony

too often
too much

I cannot
I cannot

you

I cannot touch

PERSEPHONE'S DEMISE

she was once married
by the god of hell, romanced
dearest Hades burning blue
Persephone never stood a chance

when he pulled her with his charm
suggesting, never asking
convinced her into his arms
for an aggressive unmasking

in true passionate light of red
she burned into him at last
her fateful demise was granted
a goddess, but a fool falling fast

when you dance with the devil
you will always lose yourself
his only goal is to feed his flames
to conjure purple and nothing else

something he could not do alone

GOD IS A GODDESS

who is my god, you may ask
she is a woman of glory
not a man in pompous mask
universal mother
made for creation
nurturing all life forms
earthly and alien
existence is not formed
by simply male ejaculate
it is grown carefully within
womb of woman immaculate
by the beating of her heart
the blood in her veins
this
is how you became
before you bow foolishly
to your manly god-driven ego
remember who birthed you
a feminine goddess
in her, life grows

LOCKED LOVE

I hid away my love for you
hope kept forgotten in a blue box
tucked beneath my bed while I slept
in shadows, nightmares stayed locked

once in a full moon I was tempted
to turn the key – unlatch and open
unleash the whispers from inside
my own heart, caged and broken

to my relief after much suspense
I found nothing within my cold hands
it appears our love has faded true
in his red box, I was forgotten too

no purple inside either one

176

I PRAY FOR YOU

and if I never see you again
I pray that you still smile
when she is holding your hand
I pray you reminisce a while

look in corners of her eyes for happiness
I know you will easily find it
limits in life are boundless
I know you taught me that, I admit

I believe that you will become
a greater man than you have ever been
I believe you can love peacefully
become a husband with beautiful kids

when you close your eyes in peace
at night, drift away to sleep
know that I will still meet you there
in our secret realm of dream

I'm sorry this lifetime slipped from our grasp

Uprising

rebirth
collapse first
rise again, woman
your strength grows by
adversity
fight stronger
heal your wounds
let nobody silence your
wild
we are
women of wildfires
sisters of the moon
goddesses
of night
mothers of day
daughters of the light
surviving
together now
more than ever
we ignite in universal
rebirth

*for the women
who have found themselves crumbling
left to rebuild their empires
with the pieces of yesterday
a reminder that you are becoming
more powerful than they could ever handle*

HEAR ME

I hope one day
> *can I talk to you for a moment*

all of those who were too loud
> *can I read you what I wrote*

preoccupied with themselves
> *can I tell you how I feel*

too ignorant
> *please*

to hear my muffled voice
> *I walked away and grabbed my pen*

when I wanted to speak
> *one day I will have a voice*

heads stayed bowed
> *I will show them*

eyes would never meet mine
> *what I am thinking*

I hope they pick up these pages
> *written late at night*

of silent words
> *in my books*

I hope they finally hear me
> *if they pry open the cover*

and just how much
> *of unsaid whispers*

I needed to say

IF I KNEW

if I had known you had a cage
waiting for me behind your eyes
I would have never locked your gaze
to seal my fate with yours
if I had known your arms
would become heavy chains
constricting me
when I tried to escape you
I would have never allowed them
to wrap around my body
if I had known you would penetrate me
with a knife of hellfire into my soul
disguised as a knightly sword of love
I would have never opened the doors
of my temple to you
I'm sure there were warning signs
but you managed to paint over them
with flattery before you battered me
and wore a well-fitted, versatile mask
it slipped, broken from overuse
now – I know
I saw it all
I felt it all
I survived it all
I escaped
you

SCAVENGERS

I have nothing to hide. I am not ashamed or insecure. Not of myself, not of my life. I never claimed to be perfect. I know my heart. I know my loyalty. I know my worth. I know my truth. I learned my lessons. Deception is a waste of time. I respect those who respect me and stay true to their integrity. I wake up and breathe the same air as everyone else. Some are not so lucky. Why would I not be proud to be alive after everything I've lived through? Why would I not be proud that I can still *feel* everything after everything I've lived through? This is as real as healing gets. Realising that once you find peace within yourself, you are fucking invincible. No one has the power to break you or take you anymore. Not even you. This is all me. Laying it all out messy, raw, and open. I'm tossing away the carcass of all that decays in me. Eat your hearts out, scavengers. It's a buffet.

AFFIRMATIONS

this is the reckoning
the internal epiphany of my life
where I no longer exert my energy
fighting, struggling to move forward
with that which drags me back
with who that pulls me down
I am ready to let go of those
who no longer deserve my heart
as simple as a goodbye forever
thank you for the lessons
see you again – never
I forgive but I do not forget
and I will not be sorry
for doing what is necessary
to save myself
the deserving
the good
the peace
the love
will follow
I am ready
more than ever
to finally let you go

AMNESIA

when I miss him
I am scared
I will forget the details
of his greying hair
arms around me
a protector's vice
his warm skin and honey eyes
staring into them
touching him
god damn
I could have died
with a smile
on my face – but now
I accept our fate
with memory by my side
holding back tears, a silent shout
one more wish on myself
please
don't erase him
lest I die
without

OBSIDIAN

I took your hate as jagged ore
and forged myself a pair of wings – over time
I hammered them
with the same ferocious strength
you used to beat me down with – over time
I sharpened them with the decaying irons
you caged me in – over time
I molded them with precision
by the flames you threw me into – every time
by survivor's alchemy
they became indestructible
my wings of obsidian ignited
I licked the edges to make sure
you would never again
cause me pain, delighted
I carried my wings with pride
they took years to complete
watch me glisten and glide
strengthened by the heat
I escape – soaring from your hell
throw your fire at me
as you will
it will only make my wings stronger
it will only make me
fly higher

Not Like That

look at me
she said
not with your eyes
yet he undresses
her clothes
no
hold me close
she said
he grabs her
by the throat
no
kiss me softly
she said
his lips shoot at her
like a cannon
no
touch my heart
she said
he pulls on her hair
reaches further down
no
hear me sing
she said
he raises his voice
louder
no
he doesn't understand
no
not like that

KEEP DIGGING

keep digging your own grave
deeper, deeper darling
do not complain to me
blame me
when you are left in the dark
colder than you were
when you claimed
to love me

keep digging, darling
you might find your way back to hell and warm up

A TERRIBLE HONEYMOON

a girl once fell in love with a wolfman, foolishly
most have feared, with dark eyes of dread
but this fairy tale does not end happily
enchanted rivers now flow deepened red

a mistress of wild nature at heart – fiery she was
burning of hope and adventurous desire
out of the night appeared fate's reaching paws
on a demonic hunt for rare feminine fire

a frolic of trickery through his sinister forest
sudden ravaging under black full moon
howls erupted into blood curdling chorus
his insatiable hunger to taste her doom

red cloak shredded, claws embedded
claimed flesh of woman – forcefully wedded

*This piece was written to raise awareness to the
tragedy of forced and arranged marriages. A very
terrifying reality many young girls and women have
faced around the world, and certainly not a fairy tale
or happily ever after. My prayers are with them.*

IN ANOTHER LIFETIME

he changed my life forever
for worse and for better
it would be selfish
not to thank him
for his destruction
sparked my creation
sometimes the best muse
is the one fate refused
destiny joined our paths
a journey to the moon and back
tasting heaven and hell
purgatory's curse fell
a gift of love and lesson for life
in another universe
I became his wife

thank you, 143

Overdose

with you
I could foolishly overdose
on the sound of your voice
that curls my toes
I would collect
every butterfly inside of me
that ever tried
to escape or hide
from the cage
I built around myself
to keep parts of you in mine
I could never become tired
of the growing wildfire
that sparks when you
kiss my lips
if you drowned me in desire
we would both rise higher
I could die
in a moment
of bliss

FORGIVENESS

Forgiveness is picking up the petals that lay torn apart at your feet. Ruined in a moment of rage, and realising what has been done. Maybe you are those petals. Forgiveness is burying them in hopes that flowers will bloom again. Even if the earth never breaks, you learned a lesson. You cannot put back together what has been destroyed, but you can try to grow new life from it. Forgiveness is believing in the beauty and potential of what's left. What was once beautiful will always be beautiful. When you still try to grow, that is how healing shows. Forgive yourself, forgive them. Bury your seeds in the dirt of the past. Then, you will learn how to break free towards the sun.

I HOPE HE GIVES YOU ROSES

I hope he gives you roses
I hope he lays rose petals
across your bed
before he lays you on them
I hope he gives you roses
when you are sad
and when you are happy
I hope he surprises you
with roses on a Monday night
when he apologises
I hope he gives you a dozen
I hope he goes great distances
and throws them up great heights
to reach you
I hope you keep every single one
I hope he leads you to him
along a path of red petals
and scented magic
waiting for you
on bended knee
with a ring in hand
on Christmas Eve
I hope he loves you
like you deserve
I hope he never stops
giving you roses
I hope you find him
I did once
so will you

UNTIL THEN

do not lose sleep
into the unknown
my love
everything
will fall into place
until then
rest

CARESS ME

my love
caress me sweetly
pull my hair back
gently, neatly
tell me
I am yours
my body whispers
yes
of course
let soul surrender
to sweetest sin
a wildfire coursing
deep within
giving into temptation
completely
I belong
to him

MIDNIGHT

I exhale my tempting poison
demonic darkness in every breath
suffocating perfume of evil
consumes me as I lay to rest

exorcise my heart in shadow
lend me light to fill my lungs
unchain my soul and release me
before haunting delight does come

draw my curses out with yours
let them dance, roam and fight
something wicked in our love lies
still breathing, beyond dark midnight

kiss me, let me taste your demons

WIDOW

beauty is seen in weeping eyes
even blind can still believe
there is magic when a widow cries
she keeps eternal hope alive
though she may retreat to deceive
in fear of living on her own
time will pass, love does not seize
mourning tears rebuild her home
as he whispers to her by the trees

my dear, you are never alone

HEALER

I will continue
to weave my magic
into your heart
for as long as I live
for as long as you let me
help you
I will lick your wounds
seal them with gold
to heal you
for as long as I live
for as long as you let me
love you

CROWN THE QUEEN

I want to tell you
about a little girl
who played with fire
until her world
became ignited
by the command
of her own
powerful voice

she lived in hopes of a magic dance
in a land of make-believe, dreamlike trance
ruler of her own castle quite decorated
with delicate care she illuminated
a spark of innocent beauty
would become rebellious, unruly
or so subjects said instead of elating
when she let out a roar – furiously vibrating
shattered the mosaic, glass window stain
she will erupt, collapse kingdom reign
little princess crowned herself a queen
now they bow to her – a wise woman seen
little princess
she
was me

BORN BELOW ZERO

I came into this world
screaming within a blizzard
a snowstorm as frantic
as my mother's labor pain
I came into this world
roaring like a lion
as the month does
before hail
becomes rain
I came into this world
below zero degrees
a Piscean spirit of old
heart chained
in ice – frozen
eternally trapped
in the cold

sometimes, I can't help but wonder
if my tendencies to disconnect from people
and appearing to have a cold heart
have any connection
to how I came into this world

sometimes, I can't even warm myself up
sometimes, I believe I can freeze hell over
sometimes, I am hell
sometimes, I am a blizzard

CURSED A FOOL

I must have been cursed
with the heart of a joker
mind of a misfit
soul of a sinner
body like a doormat
arms for perfect binding
so brutally obvious
that men take one look and say
jackpot – she's my prize
possess her – she's my property
trick her – she's a hopeless romantic
lie to her – she loves sweet nothings
fool her
into believing
I'm everything
she needs
before she realises
I'm everything
she doesn't
it will be too late for her
to escape
she is my prisoner
my prey

UPROOT YOURSELF

she grew tired
of trying to grow
with him
his roots
only choked hers
he was poisoning
the earth around her
he invaded her space
stole her sunlight
too often that surely
it would lead
to her withering
so, she uprooted herself
re-planted, stretched her roots
far away from him
she grew on her own
she flourished beautifully
breathed fresher air until
the wind carried her seeds away

and by the light of the sun
drinking cleansing rain
a field of wildflowers
bloomed
without pain

WILD CHILD

my wild child, you are an ember
of my own beating heart
burning amongst the stars
galaxies grow stronger as you do
I pray you never lose your spark
there is a warrior deep inside of you
a fierce, untameable soul
you were born of divine creation
I saw the future in my arms unfold
one day I know, you must roam free
you have a voice – a power
that can transform reality
set your own course, fortify your path
turn past into lesson, never look back
set fires in the twilight to Luna
and when the sun rises
unleash your magic skyward
chasing rainbows with Iris
weather all changing seasons
remind yourself gracefully
of the many reasons
your roots are destined
to keep growing
wild and free

grow your life wildly and flourish beautifully
my daughter

Forget Me Not

wherever my roots may grow
extend to or be planted
I pray they are laced with starlight
and extend to endless planes
never fertilised with poison
always humming with life
I pray my fingertips bloom marigolds
eyelids close like sleeping petals
my feet planting seeds of growth
along every surface I sow
I pray my veins sparkle beauty
carry nectar through rivers
so that I may nourish a meadow
full of wildflowers dancing
in sunlight
I pray that my garden
blossoms free
from bouquets of greed
prisons of flower pots
and you
forget me not

her petals
once were
delicately perfumed
thorns emerged
where flowers
once bloomed
scorched soil
tainted earth
brought strength
with beauty
woman's rebirth

wildflowers in bloom

DEDICATIONS

to my daughter

who will always know
how strong her roots are
so that she may plant her own garden
and grow beautifully in life and into herself

to my mother

who deserves to dance in a field of wildflowers
but is always watering everyone else's first
thank you for all of your love and support
you are my best friend

to my grandmother

who is without a doubt sprouting love
upon the heavens with her smiles and laughs
you inspired me to nurture my own life
the same way you cared for your flowers and family

*for the strongest women in my life
with all of my love – thank you*

ABOUT THE AUTHOR

Leanna Hewitt (LUNAIRIS) is a self-published author from Ontario, Canada. She is an avid writer and dedicates herself to transforming her thoughts and emotions into art.

Her writing often reflects powerful personal truths and lessons. She encourages growth, no matter what has been entangled into her roots. A lover of all things magic, she is always searching for the beauty in between love and tragedy while healing from abuse, mental illness, and loss in her life. She embraces the light and dark of all that exists. Expressing her immense pride in striving to be the best mother she can be for her daughter, she hopes to leave behind her story to remind her that her roots are strong, and she can overcome anything life and love gives her.

She describes her inspiration as erratic and unpredictable like her, thriving in ecstatic highs and chaotic lows. Drawing from thoughts, memories, experiences, emotions, and dreams, she has adapted a passion for sharing her story in hopes of inspiring others to keep surviving. She is a lover of all things romantic, astronomical, aquatic, artistic, wild, fantastic, and of course – purple.

Her poetic idols since she was a young girl include Edgar Allan Poe and William Shakespeare. They were her secret bedtime stories, reading their complete works repeatedly as a child into her teenage and adult years. They have a special place on her bookshelf and in her heart.

Her pen name, LUNAIRIS, is a tribute to the moon and Greek Goddess Iris, Goddess of the rainbow and messenger between the earth and sky.

Wildflowers in Bloom is her second collection of poetry following *Dreaming in Purple.*

all my
love
Thank you
— L

wildflowers in bloom